M000169121

HOW IRAN FUELS SYRIA WAR

DETAILS OF THE IRGC COMMAND HQ AND KEY OFFICERS IN SYRIA

NATIONAL COUNCIL OF RESISTANCE OF IRAN
US REPRESENTATIVE OFFICE

HOW IRAN FUELS SYRIA WAR; Details of the IRGC command HQ and key officers in Syria

First published in 2016 by

National Council of Resistance of Iran - U.S. Representative Office (NCRI-US), 1747 Pennsylvania Ave., NW, Suite 1125, Washington, DC 20006

ISBN-10: 1-944942-90-4
ISBN-13: 978-1-944942-90-8

Library of Congress Cataloging-in-Publication Data

National Council of Resistance of Iran - U.S. Representative Office.
How Iran Fuels Syria War; Details of the IRGC command HQ and key officers in Syria

1. Iran-Syria. 2. Syria-war. 3. Iran-military. 4. Iran-Foreign relations.
5. Security, International.

First Edition: July 2016

Printed in the United States of America

TABLE OF CONTENTS

HOW IRAN FUELS SYRIA WAR

DETAILS OF THE IRGC COMMAND HQ AND KEY OFFICERS IN SYRIA

A Look at the 5-year War in Syria

More than five years have passed since January 2011, when unrest erupted in the streets of Syria. Over the past five years, replete with war crimes and violations of international humanitarian law by the Bashar Assad regime and its closest ally, the clerical regime in Iran, later joined by Russia and others, Syria's people and nation have gone through a historic period. Hundreds of thousands of innocent Syrians have fallen, millions have been displaced, and millions more who sought refuge from neighboring countries and faraway nations endure appalling conditions. Despite the hardships, the people of Syria continue their struggle, intent on achieving victory against a united front of their enemies.

It Started Peacefully

Initially, the demand for change was peaceful. For several months after January 26, 2011, millions took to the streets of Syrian cities and villages, rallying around the central slogan "the people seek the regime's downfall." Relying on the political, financial and security support of the Iranian regime, Assad responded with bullets.

The largest anti-regime demonstration in hama, syria

Formation of Free Syrian Army

Colonel Riadh al-As'ad announced formation of FSA in August 2011

The harsh response prompted many Syrian army officers to join the popular movement, and later form the Free Syrian Army (FSA) in August 2011. Colonel Riadh al-As'ad first announced the FSA's formation, and groups of officers, military personnel and civilians joined.

Soon afterward, the FSA launched the armed struggle against the Syrian dictatorship, and Assad's forces suffered successive serious defeats. Extensive defections of army officers and commanders followed, many of whom joined the FSA. As the prospect of a revolution toppling Assad grew, the clerical regime in Iran began deploying its military

Brig. Gen. Hossein
Hamedani and Supreme
Leader Ali Khamenei

might to Syria unannounced. Iran's supreme leader Ali Khamenei dispatched Hossein Hamedani, the senior commander of the Islamic Revolutionary Guard Corps (IRGC) Mohammad Rassoul Allah Division, assigned to control and suppress Tehran. Hamedani drew on his military experience as a commander during the Iran-Iraq war, as well as on his role in suppressing the 2009 popular uprisings in Iran. At his juncture, the forces sent by the Iranian regime were primarily at the command level, as evidenced by the FSA's capture of 48 IRGC commanders two months later.

Mehdi Taeb, head of the Ammar Garrison said on February 14, 2013: "Syria is our 35th province, and is a strategic province for us. If the enemy attacks us and seeks to take Syria or Khuzestan, our priority would be to keep Syria, because if we keep Syria, we can retake Khuzistan. But if we lose Syria, we cannot keep Tehran."

Assad Uses Chemical Weapons

The struggle continued. Resistance rose to new heights, threatening to topple the Assad dictatorship. On August 21, 2013, the Assad regime signaled its willingness to go to any lengths to confront the revolutionaries and to instill fear in the populace. His forces used chemical weapons, leading to the mass murder of civilians in the suburbs around Damascus, especially in western and eastern Ghouta. Most of the victims were found to be women and children. Various international institutions later confirmed that chemical weapons had been used, but the West, and especially the U.S. government, failed to respond.

A member of the Iranian parliament, Alireza Zakani, later revealed Tehran's role in preventing a U.S. attack in response to the chemical bombardment. According to Zakani, Supreme Leader Khamenei wanted to avoid even one U.S. bullet from being fired in Syria, adding: "The Qods Force command sent a warning through a senior Iraqi official, who usually transmitted such messages to the Americans, that (if a U.S. attack on Syria took place,) America's interests and bases in the region would be targeted."

In a statement released on September 2, 2013, the National Council of Resistance of Iran revealed "The massacre of the residents of Ashraf was launched on September 1 on the direct orders of Khamenei, and carried out by forces under orders from Maliki in close cooperation with the terrorist Qods Force... In the wake of the chemical bombardment of the suburbs of Damascus and the increased possibility of a U.S. military strike, Khamenei called for urgent action against Ashraf. Qassem Soleimani, commander of the terrorist Qods Force, travelled to Iraq on Tuesday, August 27, 2013, and met with Maliki outside office hours (10:30 p.m.). The two discussed the possible U.S. military attack on Syria and the massacre at Ashraf."[1]

ISIS Emerges and Targets Syrian Opposition

Isis fighters marching in Raqqa, Syria AP

A new phenomenon emerged as the war in Syria dragged on, known as Daesh (ISIS, ISIL) and declaring Raqqa as its capital. Without doubt, ISIS is responsible for the suppression of the peoples of Iraq and Syria by the mullahs with the help of Assad and Maliki, a subject requiring a separate study. U.S. Secretary of State John Kerry said in an interview

---

[1]   On September 1, 2013, in the early hours, at the behest of the Iranian regime, Iraqi forces attacked Camp Ashraf, killing 52 residents, and kidnapping seven in a massacre widely condemned by the U.S. Government and senior Members of Congress. No one was ever held accountable for this crime. See: http://www.state.gov/r/pa/prs/ps/2013/09/213696.htm

"ISIS was created by Assad releasing 1,500 prisoners from jail and Maliki releasing 1,000 people in Iraq who were put together as a force of terror types."[2]

The mullahs' regime made use of its experience in suppression and control within Iran. Tehran's Ministry of Intelligence alongside the IRGC Intelligence Organization trained Assad's security forces in all their dirty tactics and tricks. Working closely with the Tehran regime's agents, Assad's security forces began plotting how to create rifts within the opposition groups and assassinate political figures.

According to reports from within the Iranian Intelligence Ministry, working closely with Assad's security forces the Ministry drew up two plans: the first called the Infiltration Project, to instill division and dissent into the opposition; and the second called the Knapsack Project, to bring about armed clashes between the groups and the tribes.

Major Victories of Syrian Opposition in 2015

The first half of 2015 brought another watershed moment in the 5-year campaign for democracy by the Syrian people. In the early months of 2015 until roughly the middle of the year, armed Syrian opposition forces scored major victories on the northern and southern frontiers. These were significant setbacks for the opposing camp of Assad forces, Hezbollah fighters and the Iranian regime's agents. The advancement of opposition forces, especially in Idlib, Jisr al-Shughur, and the al-Ghab Plain, and the marshaling of forces toward the coast and Latakia heralded the potential downfall of the Assad regime. This coincided with the series of defeats experienced

---

[2]   Interview With Gregory Palkot of Fox News, November 17, 2015, available on State Department website http://www.state.gov/secretary/remarks/2015/11/249588.htm

by Assad's forces in Daraa. It was at this point that the Iranian regime felt the need to make a plea to Russia.

Russia Gets Involved

Russia's active entry into the Syrian war at the end of September 2015 opened a new chapter in the conflict. The Iranian regime's Qods Force commander Qassem Soleimani had previously committed in a meeting with Russian President Vladimir Putin in Moscow that if Russia were to provide sufficient air support, the IRGC and its allied forces would be able to quickly advance on the ground and retake territory from the opposition. The arrangement was confirmed once again during a meeting between Putin and Khamenei in Tehran. Khamenei vowed to Putin that he would fight in Syria to his last IRGC soldier.

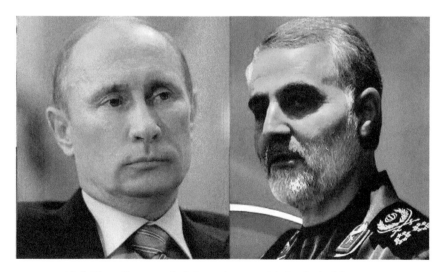

Maj. Gen. Qassem Soleimani met with Putin in Moscow

The IRGC Doubles its Forces in Syria

The first round of the IRGC attacks, codenamed the "Moharram Operation," failed without producing significant results. During this period, Hussein Hamedani, Commander in Chief of the IRGC in Syria, and a large number of other IRGC generals were killed. Nevertheless, in December 2015, Khamenei ordered the IRGC to stand fast in the Aleppo region. He reiterated that if they retreated, their fate would be similar to the Iran-Iraq war and the regime would ultimately be defeated in Syria. Thus, in January 2016, the IRGC doubled the number of its forces in Syria to about 60,000 and launched extensive attacks in the region. However, despite tactical advances in some areas, these forces have been unable to even take control of southern Aleppo.

Maj Gen. Qassem Soleimani talking to troops in Aleppo

IRGC Plans for Capturing Aleppo

Tehran remained unable to advance its agenda in Aleppo and the IRGC faced a deadlock. In March 2016, Khamenei ordered the regular

Army's 65th Division (special operations) to be deployed around Aleppo, and increased the number of other forces as well. Plans for a major offensive to capture Aleppo were set in motion. During attacks by the IRGC and the Iranian army in April 2016, dozens of the regime's forces, including IRGC commanders and staff, Iranian army personnel and foreign mercenaries from Iraq, Lebanon and Afghanistan, were killed. In late May and early June 2016, the IRGC forces south of Aleppo and Khan Touman suffered several blows. At present, opposition forces have retaken control of areas in the south and north of the province of Aleppo and Latakia. Reports indicate there are discussions within the Tehran regime of the probable defeat of the IRGC's entire siege of Aleppo.

Although the IRGC and the Iranian regime's regular army forces have failed to change the balance of military power in Syria, Khamenei insists on sending more IRGC and army forces into the Syrian quagmire. Seeing no way forward, and no way back.

SUMMARY OF THE EXTENT OF TEHRAN'S REGIME'S MEDDLING IN THE SYRIAN WAR

I n truth, at the present time the Iranian regime in its entirety is invested in the war in Syria. It is employing all its resources and capabilities. Despite the massive scale of its involvement, however, it is militarily at an impasse. The following points are indicative of the regime's all-out effort:

1. Khamenei is personally making the decision on all relevant matters, whether political or military. On some occasions, he is even deciding military tactics. In meetings with the regime's ambassadors in November 2015, with Vladimir Putin in December 2015, and with commanders of the regime's Army in a public meeting in April 2016, he stressed the need to

continue the war effort and preserve the Assad dictatorship, vowing to fight to the last man.

2. Khamenei has involved the top level of his regime's military command. For example, IRGC General Mohammad Ali Jafari, the IRGC's Commander in Chief, personally travelled to Syria for the offensives against the cities of Nubl and Al Zahraa in February 2016. IRGC General Mohsen Reza'i, who was commander in chief during the Iran-Iraq War, was appointed Khamenei's Deputy for the Syrian War in 2016, a post he retains today. IRGC General Qassem Soleimani, Commander of the IRGC Qods Force, regularly travels to Syria and meets with Bashar Assad.

3. Although the IRGC's Qods Force remains its primary extraterritorial fighting force, and the primary force in Syria, the IRGC's ground forces as well as those of the regular Iranian Army have also been deployed and are fully engaged in the war effort. The IRGC has a troop quota for every Iranian province for replacements to send to Syria for the units stationed there. Other IRGC forces, such as naval and air forces, are also involved. In 2016, Khamenei for the first time ordered the formation of airborne units within the IRGC's ground forces, to better equip them for their onslaught into Syria.

4. More than 70,000 non-Iranian and Iranian forces have been deployed by the IRGC to fight in Syria. That exceeds the number of Syrian military forces. According to IRGC reports, the Syrian military has less than 50,000 troops.

5. In addition to its military forces, the mullahs' regime has also involved the personnel of its embassies and government agencies in the war effort. For example, IRGC General Rostam Qassemi is overseeing logistical support for the Syrian war and is the representative of the Khatem Garrison. Previously, he was the commander of the Khatem Garrison as well as Oil

Minister under the Ahmadinejad administration. Moreover, the IRGC is the key player in the Iranian economy, and is also able to use its vast resources and wealth to further its war strategy.

6. Over the past 5 years, the Tehran regime has budgeted about 100 billion dollars for the war, most of it sent to Syria under cover from Khamenei's office to expedite its dispatch. The funds are spent on purchases of military weaponry and on the Syrian military's expenses. The Tehran regime spends one billion dollars annually in Syria solely on the salaries of the forces affiliated with the IRGC, including military forces, militias, and Shiite networks.

7. Iran's ruling regime has deployed a vast network of its mullahs to Syria, where their warmongering stirs up the fighters. And much like during the Iran/Iraq War, religious zealots are also sent to Syria to fuel the flames of religious fervor among the IRGC's Basiij fighters and Afghan and Iraqi mercenaries.

A large number of top IRGC commanders with ranks of general and colonel have been killed in Syria. To advance its war strategy, Tehran has been obliged to dispatch commanders from the Iran/Iraq War era, many of whom have been killed. Total figures on the number killed from the ranks of the IRGC, and from Syrian, Afghan and Iraqi militias (excluding Syrian military forces) exceed 10,000, of whom 1500 were Iranian members of the IRGC.

Russia's President Vladimir Putin met supreme
leader Ali Khamenei in Tehran

Syrian President Assad travels to Tehran to meet
with supreme leader Ali Khamenei

THE IRGC DIVIDES SYRIA INTO MILITARY ZONES

The IRGC has divided Syria into five fronts. The Syrian army's role has essentially been denigrated to a secondary or supportive function in the conflict. The attacks and assault operations are conducted by the IRGC forces and their mercenaries.

These five zones include[3]:

1) The central command center;
2) The southern front;
3) The middle front;
4) The northern front; and
5) The coastal front.

The eastern front, a relatively large and desolate area, is controlled by Daesh; IRGC forces do not have a presence in that region.

Below are some of the details about the centers and circumstances of the IRGC's presence in each of these fronts.

---

[3]   These five areas have been color-coded on the full map of Syria.

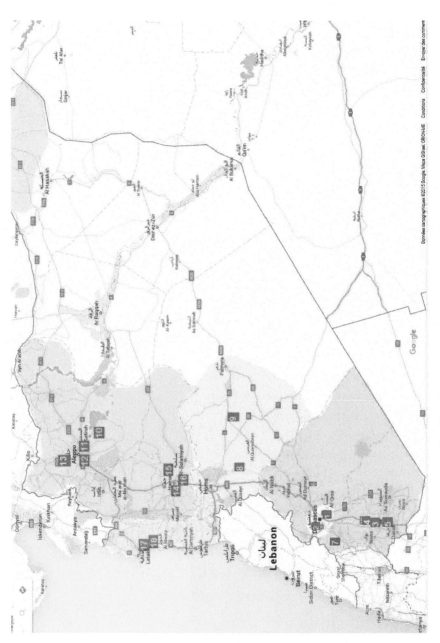

The IRGC has divided Syria into five fronts

The Central Command Centers[4]

1 - The Glass Building (*Maghar Shishe'i*): The main IRGC command center in Syria is a location called the Glass Building, adjacent to the Damascus Airport. The IRGC placed its command center near the airport after assessing that the airport would be the last location to fall. IRGC forces airlifted to Syria are dispatched to other areas from this location. One of the commanders stationed at the Glass Building is IRGC Brig. Gen. Seyyed Razi Mousavi, commander of IRGC Quds Force logistics in Syria. Between 500 and 1,000 Revolutionary Guards are stationed there.

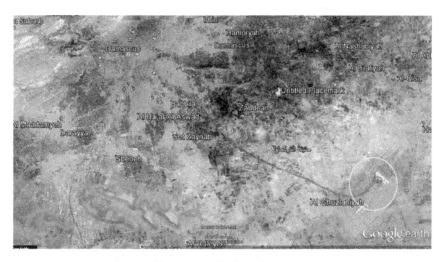

General location of The Glass Building

---

[4]   Damascus and its suburbs are considered included in this zone

The Glass Building

2 - Shibani Garrison (aka Imam Hossein Garrison): This garrison is located in the Shibani region, northwest of Damascus towards Zabadani. Assad's Republican Guards were previously stationed there. The IRGC calls it the Imam Hossein Garrison. It has a capacity of 6,000 forces, but currently some 3,000 IRGC forces, including the commando brigade of the 19th Fajr Division from Shiraz, Afghan forces known as the Fatemiyoun, and Lebanese Hezbollah are stationed there. This garrison acts as the support force to protect Assad's palace and the expeditionary force against possible attacks from Zabadani by the Syrian regime's opponents. This garrison is used to dispatch forces to other fronts. For example, in April 2016, four battalions of the Afghan Fatemiyoun force were dispatched to Palmyra from this location.

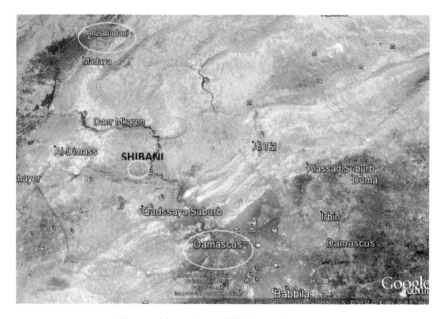

General location of Shibani Garrison

Shibani Garrison

The command center, Red Villa inside Shibani Garrison

IRGC Centers at the Southern Front[5]

3 - Base 18000 (aka Zeinab Garrison): This site is a former university situated 45 kilometers from Damascus on the route to Daraa. The IRGC's armored units and some of Syria's National Defense Forces (pro-Assad militia) are stationed here, in addition to some of the IRGC logistic and support units and Fatemiyoun.

Base 18000 and Yarmouk base

Base 18000

---

[5]   Parts of Rief, Damascus, Daraa, al-Qunaitra, and as-Suwayda provinces are included in this zone

4 - Yarmouk Base: This base is a short distance from Base 18000. Some of the IRGC and Lebanese Hezbollah forces are stationed there.

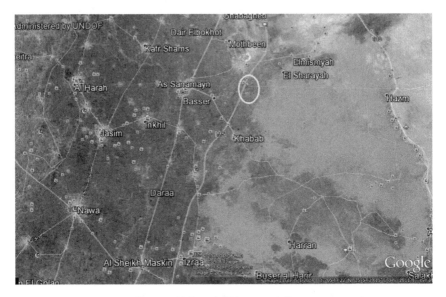

General View of Yarmouk base

Yarmouk Base

5 - Izra Base: The IRGC has a base near the city of Izra, where air defense units equipped with SAM-1 (surface-to-air) missiles are stationed. The IRGC forces have been told in briefings that this base is tasked with defense against possible Israeli air raids. Missile units from Shiraz's al-Mahdi Division and units from the IRGC's aerospace section are stationed here. The base is actually made up of two missile sites close to each other. Other IRGC units who are tasked with carrying out operations in southern Syria or near the Jordanian border use this base as the barracks for their troops.

General View of Izra base

Izra missile base

Second Izra missile base

6 - Al-Dumayr Military Airbase - Third Corps Base: IRGC forces are stationed in this airbase, which used to be a military airport for the Syrian army. The airbase is located 50 kilometers from the Syrian capital off the Damascus-Baghdad Highway, near the village of Al-Dumayr. The IRGC uses this base to assemble its forces operating in the middle zone.

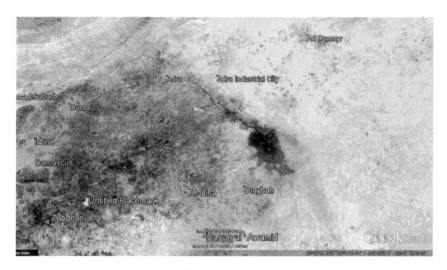

General area of Al-Dumayr Military Airbase

Al-Dumayr Military Airbase

7 – Naba' al-Fawar Garrison: This garrison is based in the Ghonaitareh region, south of Damascus and is located near Sa'sa and 15 km from the Golan Heights. The Hezbollah controls this garrison, where the IRGC forces are also present. Reports say that about 2,000 IRGC and Hezbollah forces are based there.

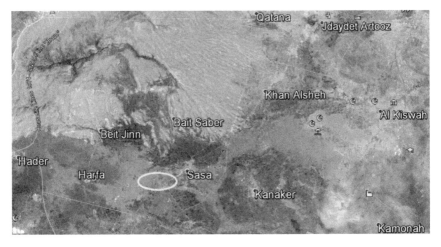

Al Favar Military Base

IRGC Centers at the Middle Front

This zone can be divided into the two middle and eastern sections with the IRGC having no presence in the latter. It includes Homs province where IRGC forces are stationed. Hasakah and Deir ez-Zor provinces are also part of this front but IRGC forces do not have a presence there.

8 - **Shairat Airbase:** Three battalions of the IRGC are stationed in the Homs region. Military flights take off from this airbase.

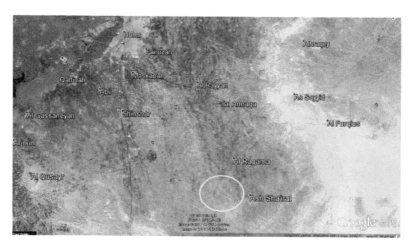

General area of Shairat airbase

Shairat airbase

9 - T4 Military Airbase: This airbase, which belongs to the Syrian army, is located 50 kilometers from Palmyra. The IRGC has used it as a concentration point in staging attacks on Palmyra. In October 2015, more than 1,000 IRGC forces were stationed there. According to one report received, around 1,000 Russian commandos were seen at this airbase in October 2015.

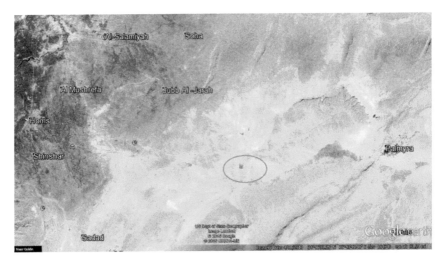

General area of T4 airbase

T4 airbase

IRGC Centers at the Northern Front

The region extends from the city of Hama to the border with Turkey, and includes the Aleppo and Idlib provinces. This is the most important front for the IRGC in the Syrian war.

10 - Bohouth Garrison (aka Ruqiya): This garrison, which is located southeast of al-Safirah city situated in the east of Aleppo, was part of the Bohouth (investigation) complex of the Syrian army (codenamed 350). The IRGC has labelled this garrison the Ruqiya base. This garrison is situated behind the main frontline forces in southern Aleppo.

According to eyewitness accounts, in early 2016, about 2,000-3,000 forces from the IRGC and Afghan, Iraqi and Lebanese Hezbollah mercenaries were stationed there. The material for chemical weapons and missile fuel are produced at this garrison.

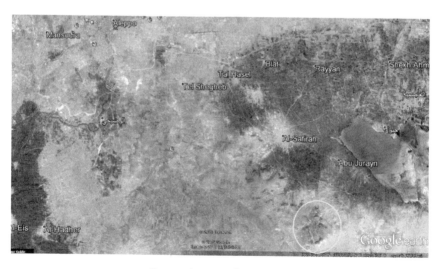

General area of Bohouth

Bohouth Garrison

Bohouth Garrison Command HQ1

Bohouth Garrison Command HQ2

11. Aleppo Airport: The Aleppo Airport is controlled by the Syrian Army and the IRGC. The IRGC visits the location using planes and helicopters, which is why it has its own dedicated base in this airport.

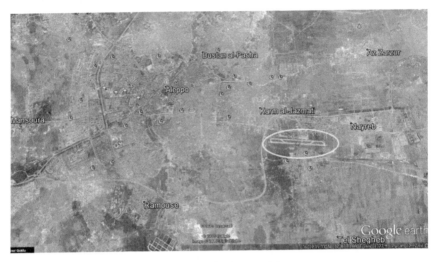

General area of Aleppo Airport

Aleppo Airport

12. Assad Academy Garrison: This command base is located in the Assad Academy northeast of Aleppo at the exit towards Hama. An elite IRGC battalion is stationed here. The military academy has been evicted and the base has been handed over to the IRGC.

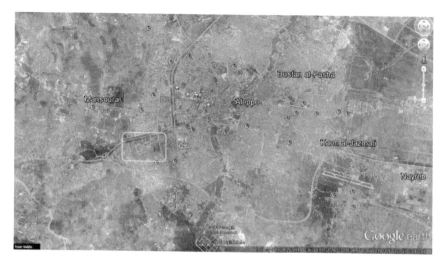

General area of Assad Academy

Assad Academy

13 – Hama Airport: The Syrian Army and the IRGC control this airport, which the IRGC uses to airlift its forces and weapons. It has a number of forces stationed at the airport.

Hama Airport

14 - Mojanzarat Base: This base, located near Salimeh village, some 3-4 kilometers from Tibat Turki village, houses the majority of the regime's forces – around 2,000. Mojanzarat is considered a secure military installation for the IRGC and army. Forces are dispatched from here to south-eastern Aleppo.

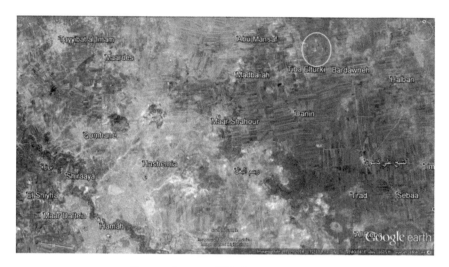

General area of Mojanzarat Base

Mojanzarat Base

15 - The Headquarters for the 47th Armored Division (near Abudarda mountain): This location was previously the headquarters for the 47th armored division of the Syrian Army. It is situated seven kilometers to the south of Serhin village. Several Guards Corps battalions are stationed there.

General area of Abu Darda

Abu Darda

16 - Mayer City Base: Following the occupation of the towns of Nubl and Al-Zahraa by the IRGC, the town of Mayer, just outside of Nubl, has been transformed into a military town under IRGC control. Residents have been evicted and are not allowed to enter. The IRGC command and control has been stationed in the town, defended by IRGC and Fatemiyoun forces.

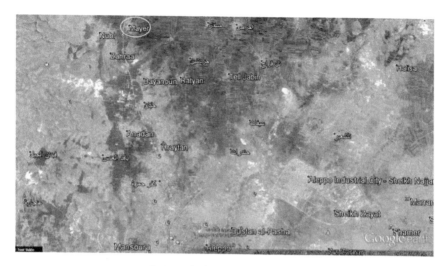

General area of Mayer City

Mayer City

IRGC Centers at the Coastal Front[6]

17 - Camp Tala'e (Shabibeh): After Russian forces arrived at Latakia airport, a significant portion of IRGC forces were transferred to the Tala'eh or *Shabiheh* Garrison. In addition to the *Syrian forces*, some 2,000 IRGC forces are present in this camp, which can house up to a total of 6,000. The IRGC dispatches its forces from this camp to Jabal al-Akrad and Jabal al-Turkeman, which are conflict areas north of Latakia.

General area of Shabibeh

Shabibeh Garrison

---

[6]   Including Latakia province and Tartus.

18 - The Hmeimim Airport: This airport is controlled by the Syrian Army and the IRGC. The IRGC uses the location to transfer logistics and also as a transit point to move forces to the northern front.

General area of Hmeimim Airport

Hmeimim Airport

THE SCOPE AND STRUCTURE OF THE IRANIAN REGIME'S FORCES IN SYRIA

The Iranian regime is at an impasse in Syria, but given Khamenei's insistence on a military victory, it views the solution as increasing its presence and involvement, in the hope that a way can be found to keep Assad in power. Especially after the start of the Iranian New Year in March 2016, the IRGC increased its forces according to a previously drawn up plan and, on Khamenei's orders, the Regular Army dispatched its special operations forces. The estimate of the total number of the Iranian regime's forces (i.e. non-Syrians) in Syria reached more than 70,000.

The composition of these forces is as follows:

IRGC forces:	8,000 to 10,000
Iranian Regular Army:	5,000 to 6,000
Non-Iranian mercenaries:	
• **Iraqi militias:**	Around 20,000 (from 10 groups)
• **Afghan militias (Fatemiyoun):**	15,000 to 20,000
• **Lebanese Hezbollah:**	7,000 to 10,000
• **Militias from Pakistan (Zeinabiyoun), Palestine, and elsewhere:**	5,000 to 7,000

The figures regarding foreign militias fluctuate. For example, some of the Iraqi militias returned home to be replaced by other Iraqi forces.

Based on specific reports from within the IRGC, the forces of the Syrian regular army number less than 50,000 across the country. Therefore, in addition to their command function, even in terms of the sheer number of forces, the Iranian regime's forces and mercenaries outnumber Assad's own forces in Syria.

ORGANIZATIONAL CHART OF THE IRANIAN REGIME'S COMMAND FORCES IN SYRIA

This chart includes the various branches of the IRGC, such as ground, air, navy, and missile forces, and foreign militias, including Iraqi, Afghani, Lebanese Hezbollah, Pakistani and Indian mercenaries organized in the Zeynabioun battalions, in addition to other regime forces in other countries. (The chart is attached). Note that the chart does not include the Iranian army's organizational structure.

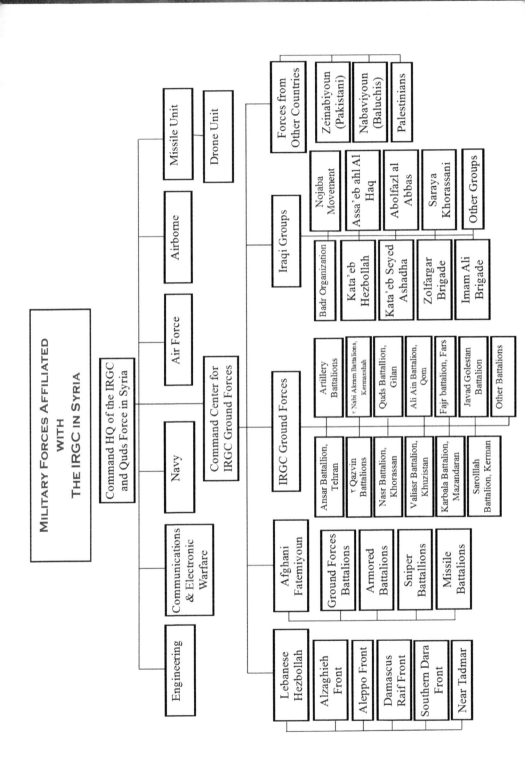

DETAILS OF THE IRGC COMMAND STRUCTURE & INDIVIDUAL COMMANDERS

B rig. General Hossein Hamedani was the commander of all Iranian forces in Syria, until he was killed on October 7, 2015. Since then, the command of the regime's forces in Syria has been assigned to a Command Council, whose members include: IRGC Brig. Gen. Esmail Qaani (deputy of Qassem Soleimani who is the commander of the Quds Force) and IRGC Brig. Gen. Mohammad Jafaar Assadi (aka Seyyed Ahmad Madani). After Hamedani was killed, IRGC Brig. Gen. Assadi was nominally named commander, but more recently changes were under consideration.

Some of the top IRGC commanders in Syria include Brig. Gen. Seyyed Razi Mousavi--former commander of the Quds Force in Syria and currently the Quds Force logistics commander there; IRGC Brig. Gen. Fallahpour--head of IRGC counter-intelligence in Syria; IRGC Brig. Gen. Majid Alavi (a pseudonym) -- a deputy to Qassem Soleimani; and IRGC Brig. Gen. Abu Heydar (a pseudonym) -- a commander of the foreign militias and deputy to Soleimani. Brig. Gen. Seyyed Javad, has been responsible for commanding the IRGC's forces in the northern front.

In the new Iranian year (March 2016), Khamenei appointed IRGC Major General Mohsen Reza'i as advisor to the Iranian regime's operational command for Syria. Reza'i was a commander of the IRGC during the Iran-Iraq war.

IRGC Brig. Gen. Esmail Qaani

IRGC Brig. Gen. Mohammad Jafaar Assadi

IRGC Major General Mohsen Rezai

THE IRANIAN REGIME'S FINANCIAL INVESTMENT

I n order to ensure the survival of the Assad regime, the Iranian regime has been forced to commit a significant amount of money. These astonishing expenditures reveal the extent to which the clerical regime is prepared to go. Although exact figures have not been revealed, there are various reports in this regard. It is estimated that over the course of the 5-year conflict in Syria, Tehran has spent about 15-20 billion dollars a year, totaling somewhere between 80 to 100 billion dollars over the 5 years.

Salaries for the Mercenaries and Agents

The regime pays salaries to foreign forces fighting in Syria, including its own IRGC personnel, Iraqi mercenaries working with the Qods Force, Afghans of the so-called Fatemiyoun, the Lebanese Hezbollah, and Pakistani forces of the so-called Zeynabioun. According to credible reports, the regime pays $1,550 to the IRGC's Iraqi mercenaries who are dispatched to Syria for a period of a month-and-a-half. If this figure is extrapolated for the regime's 70,000-strong force, then it can be estimated that Tehran pays $70,000,000 in salaries for non-Syrian forces involved in the conflict.

The Iranian regime also pays the salaries of the so-called Syrian National Defense militias. It is estimated that each member gets a monthly salary of about $100 to $200. Therefore, on average ($150 per person), and for a total of about 50,000 to 70,000 militia members tied to the IRGC in Syria, the Iranian regime pays out roughly $9,000,000 per month.

Tehran also pays families of its affiliates killed in Syria, including Syrian nationals, IRGC members, and its Iraqi, Lebanese and Afghan mercenaries. There have been over 10,000 casualties. The salaries paid to Syrian casualties are different from non-Syrians (Iranian, Afghan and Iraqi). Family members of slain Syrian forces receive roughly $40/month, while families of non-Syrian casualties receive a salary of about $500/month. If an average of $200 is considered for these casualties, the regime pays about $2,000,000 to the families of its forces killed during the Syrian conflict.

In addition to these expenses, Iran's clerical regime pays the displaced Shiites it protects after their forced expulsion or for those living in Shiite areas supported by the regime. For every family member, the regime pays roughly 4,000 Syrian Lira ($10). For example, in the cities of Nubl and al-Zahraa, the regime continued to pay money to about 35,000 individuals for several years. The total number of Shiites who are protected by the Iranian regime exceeds 100,000 people. Therefore, Tehran pays about $1,000,000/month for these individuals.

As illustrated by the above figures, to advance its agenda in Syria, the Iranian regime is financially supporting over 250,000 people. These salaries amount to anywhere between $80,000,000 to $90,000,000 per month, or about $1B over the course of a year.

Clearly, these salaries are only a small portion of the regime's overall expenses in Syria, and do not include the financial backing or the military and logistical support afforded to the Syrian army. In addition, according to reports obtained from inside the Iranian regime, Khamenei has agreed to shoulder 25% of the total costs for weapons imported to Syria from Russia.

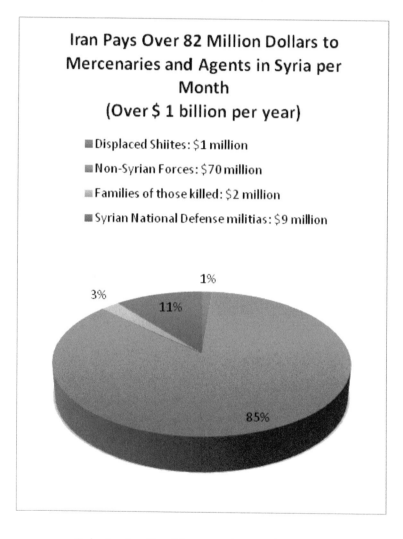

Salaries for the Mercenaries and Agents

THE IRANIAN REGIME'S CASUALTIES IN SYRIA

The number of casualties among forces tied to the Iranian regime and IRGC is very high, exceeding 10,000. According to reports obtained from inside the IRGC, the number of casualties among the IRGC and its Afghan and Iraqi mercenaries surpass 3,000. The death toll among IRGC forces in Syria prompted senior IRGC commanders to ask Khamenei to also dispatch regular army forces in order to ward off disenchantment among IRGC personnel. Khamenei was forced to accept this request, despite opposition from senior army commanders. Casualties among regular army forces over the course of the past two months have also been very high. Many of the regime's dead are buried in Syria to avoid opposition to the war or loss of moral among IRGC forces.

Statistics regarding Lebanese Hezbollah casualties stand around 2,000. The death toll has revived internal protests within the group's ranks. Hezbollah has told the IRGC that the number of casualties and defections now exceeds the number of new recruits, which has upset the group's stability.

5,000 to 7,000 forces from the Syrian militias organized by the IRGC have also been killed during this period. Their families receive money from the Iranian regime's Shahid (Martyr) Foundation and the Assistance Committee (*Komiteh Emdad*).

A large number of commanders of the IRGC and other organizations affiliated with the regime have been killed in Syria.

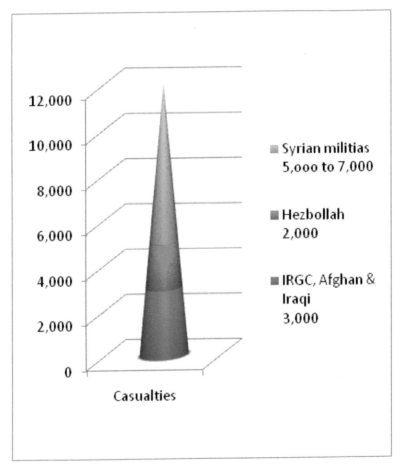

Casualties of IRGC-Affiliated Forces in Syria

Partial List of IRGC Generals Killed in Syria

IRGC Brigadier General Hassan Shateri February 2012	IRGC Brigadier General Sayed Hamid Tabataba'I Mehr February 2013

IRGC Brigadier General Haj Esmail Heydari August 2013	IRGC Brigadier General Mohammad Jamali Paghal'eh November 2013

IRGC Brigadier General
Dadollah Sheibani
June 2014

IRGC Brigadier General
Jabar Darisavi
October 2014

IRGC Brigadier General
Mohammad Ali Allahdadi
January 2015

IRGC Brigadier General
Alireza Tavassoli
(Fatemiyoun group)
February 2015

IRGC Brigadier General
Hossein Badpa
April 2015

IRGC Brigadier General
Hadi Kajbaf
April 2015

IRGC Brigadier General
Roozbeh Halisia'i
April 2015

IRGC Brigadier General
Haj Abdullah Eskandari
June 2015

IRGC Brigadier General
Hamid Mokhtarband
October 2015

IRGC Brigadier General
Jabbar Araghi
October 2015

IRGC Brigadier General
Mohammad Ali Allahdadi
October 2015

IRGC Brigadier General
Ezatollah Soleimani
October 2015

IRGC Brigadier General Farshad Hossouni Nejad October 2015	IRGC Brigadier General Abdolreza Mojiri November 2015

IRGC Brigadier General Hossein Fada'ei (Fatemiyoun group) December 2015	IRGC Brigadier General Saeed Saiyah Taheri January 2016

IRGC Brigadier General Sattar Ourang February 2016	IRGC Brigadier General Hassan Razzaqi February 2016

IRGC Brigadier General
Hamid Reza Ansari
February 2016

IRGC Brigadier General
Reza Farzaneh
March 2016

IRGC Brigadier General
Hassanali Shamsabadi
March 2016

IRGC Brigadier General
Mohsen Qajarian
March 2016

IRGC Brigadier General
Mashallah Shamseh
April 2016

IRGC Brigadier General
Javad Durbin
May 2016

IRGC Brigadier General Seyed Shafi'e Shafi'ee May 2016	IRGC Brigadier General JahangirJafarinia June 2016

IRGC Brigadier General Mohammad Hassan Hakimi (Fatemiyoun group) June 2016	IRGC Brigadier General Reza Rostami Moghadam June 2016

Partial List of IRGC Commanders Killed in Syria

IRGC Col. Amirreza Alizadeh February 2012 	IRGC Colonel Abbas Abullahi February 2015 
IRGC Colonel Qassem Gharib July 2015 	IRGC Colonel Karim Ghavabesh July 2015 

IRGC Colonel
Moslem Khizab
October 2015

IRGC Colonel
Mostafa Sadrzadeh
October 2015

IRGC Colonel
Esmail Khanzadeh
November 2015

IRGC Colonel
Mohammad Reza Alikhani
November 2015

IRGC Col.
Abdorreza Rashvand
November 2015

IRGC Colonel
Mohammad Tahaan
November 2015

IRGC Colonel
Sattar Mahmoudi
November 2015

IRGC Colonel
Ghassem Teymouri
December 2015

IRGC Colonel
Morteza Torabi Kamel
February 2016

IRGC Colonel
Asghar Fallahatpisheh
February 2016

IRGC Colonel
Hamzeh Kazemi
February 2016

IRGC Col.
AbdolHossein Sa'adatKhah
February 2016

IRGC Col.
Ahmad Goudarzi
March 2016

IRGC Colonel
Mohsen Mandani
March 2016

IRGC Col.
Ali Taheri Torshizi
March 2016

Lt. Colonel (Army)
Morteza Zarharan
April 2016

Colonel (Army)
Mojtba Zolfaghar Nasab
April 2016

IRGC Colonel
Saeed Shamloo
May 2016

IRGC Colonel Mohammad Babolsi May 2016	IRGC Colonel Rahim Kaboli May 2016

IRGC Colonel Ali Mansouri June 2016	IRGC Col. Qodratollah Abdian June 2016

8

CHAPTER

THE WAY FORWARD

The world today, especially the Middle East region, is grappling with perilous challenges and catastrophes. Sadly, the scope of this problem transcends borders and it has effectively become a global issue.

In the Middle East, countries like Syria, Iraq, and Yemen are facing catastrophic wars head on, placing them on the brink of complete devastation. But, in addition to exporting terrorism to European countries and even the United States, these hotspots are also sources of global humanitarian crises. The slaughter of 400,000 innocent Syrians, the displacement of millions more in that country and the wave of immigrants have touched off humanitarian, social, and security challenges in other countries.

It would not be an over exaggeration to claim that the Middle East can now trigger a wider global conflict.

In view of all this, clearly, governments, international organizations and every responsible human being are looking for solutions and an end to this crisis. Naturally, this can be achieved if we could discover the sources and main causes for the crisis. Various theories have been brought forward. For example, some tend to think that the source of all this lies in the religious divide or conflict between Sunnis and Shiites. Or, in view of the horrific crimes committed by the Islamic

State (ISIS or Daesh), others believe that the first step would be to eradicate ISIS. Yet the formation of ISIS is itself a component and byproduct of this catastrophic crisis that is at the heart of the problem.

The summary findings of this book, which are based on reliable information and intelligence as opposed to purely political analysis, show that if we consider the Syrian conflict, which represents the largest active hotspot of this crisis, we would immediately discover that it has been the entrance of the ruling tyrannical mullahs in Tehran that has created the current circumstances in Syria. Otherwise, the Syrian crisis had a local solution and the Syrian people would have been able to uproot Bashar Assad by relying on their popular protests initially launched five years ago and by continuing it. Undoubtedly, any outcome of this process would have been better suited for Syria than what we see today. Therefore, we can clearly say that the start, intensification and prolonging of the Syrian crisis all result from the clerical regime's presence in that country.

Put simply, therefore, the real solution before all else is to remove the Iranian factor from the scene. In the absence of the Iranian regime, which was also instrumental in pushing Russia to play a greater role in the situation, there would have been a political solution that could include the removal of Assad from power. This is because the moderate opposition is prepared to engage in negotiations and to find a political solution that can be agreed upon by all sides.

The Iranian regime is the only side that: has marshaled 70,000 forces and members and commanders of the Islamic Revolutionary Guard Corps (IRGC) and mercenaries from other countries into Syria; spent $100B to continue the war; is paying monthly salaries to over 250,000 militias and agents to prolong the conflict; has effectively engaged in the military occupation of Syria, dividing the country into 5 zones of conflict and establishing command, logistics and operations centers – 18 of which have been outlined in this book – and is obstructing a solution that includes the removal of Bashar Assad from power.

This conclusion can be similarly drawn in Yemen, Iraq, Bahrain, and Lebanon. The emergence of the mullahs' regime as a regional player has brought the Middle East to the current boiling point. Therefore, the solution can be summarized in the following:

1. The key to prudently resolving the Syrian conflict and ending this century's greatest humanitarian catastrophe is to end the occupation of the Iranian clerical regime in Syria. So long as IRGC forces remain in Syria, the country would not see peace and calm.The international community must be focused on ending Iranian regime's intervention in and occupation of Syria.

2. So long as the Iranian regime is not excluded from international negotiations, such negotiations will not be productive, as this regime is the main source of expansion of conflict in Syria and in the region.

3. The fight against ISIS will not succeed, so long as the IRGC and its agents continue to operate in Syria and Iraq, because the Iranian regime adds fuel to the sectarian violence and paves the way for the expansion of ISIS.

4. Broad-based political and financial backing to the democratic Syrian opposition, and supplying them with their essential military needs and weapons are needed.

5. Establishing a no-fly zone in northern Syria to protect the civilians and provide help to displaced refugees.

CPSIA information can be obtained at www.ICGtesting.com
Printed in the USA
BVOW05s0704210816

459678BV00016B/41/P